Feminist Bird Club
est. 2016

The Feminist Bird Club's

BIRDING *for a*

BETTER WORLD

A Guide to Finding Joy and Community in Nature

Molly Adams
and
Sydney Golden Anderson

PA PRESS

PRINCETON ARCHITECTURAL PRESS · NEW YORK

To all future birders

Published by
Princeton Architectural Press
A division of Chronicle Books LLC
70 West 36th Street
New York, NY 10018
www.papress.com

ISBN 978-1-7972-2333-9

Editor: Holly La Due
Designer: Natalie Snodgrass
Cover Design: Paul Wagner

Cover Illustration: Jen Lobo
FBC logo design: Aidan Koch

Library of Congress Control Number: 2023931677

CONTENTS

CHAPTER ONE

The Basics of Birding

CHAPTER TWO

Better Birding

CHAPTER THREE

Birding with Care

CHAPTER FOUR

Birding Together

Welcome

Birding is for all of us. That ethos has remained the bedrock of Feminist Bird Club since its formation in 2016.
If you are a member of one of the thirty (and growing) chapters around the world, it is so nice to have you. Thank you for being such an important part of this book. If you are new to Feminist Bird Club, we couldn't be more excited to embark on this journey together.

FEMINIST BIRD CLUB
2016

FEMINIST BIRD CLUB
2017

FEMINIST BIRD CLUB
2018

FEMINIST BIRD CLUB
2019

FEMINIST BIRD CLUB
2020

FEMINIST BIRD CLUB
2021

FEMINIST BIRD CLUB
2022

FEMINIST BIRD CLUB
2023

WHAT IS FEMINIST BIRD CLUB?

Feminist Bird Club (FBC) is a New York–based non-profit founded by Molly Adams in 2016 to leverage her passion for birds and social justice into a cohesive whole. The club started as a very small group of birders in Brooklyn that met monthly in local parks or at abortion-access events across New York City. Since then, FBC has expanded around the so-called United States, Canada, and Europe, with three "sibling" clubs in Central and South America.

The club was created to amplify grassroots solutions to issues in birding and break down barriers for new birders, Black people, Indigenous people, and people of color (BIPOC), LGBTQIA+ communities, people with disabilities, and women of any and all intersecting identities. In 2020, we transitioned into a nonprofit organization to legally expand our capacity to fundraise, which has been a major part of our purpose since our founding. Each year, Molly has collaborated with different artists on FBC patch designs highlighting different bird species. The patches are sold to raise funds for various organizations dedicated to abortion access, Indigenous health and wellness, ending abuse toward trans and intersex people in prisons, and more. Feminist Bird Club has been able to donate over $100,000 (US) to causes we admire thanks to revenue earned from selling patches and merchandise, bird-a-thons, and other fundraising efforts across its chapters. You can find a comprehensive list of the incredible organizations we work to support at www.feministbirdclub.org/our-work.

Feminist Bird Club's mission is forever and always rooted in an unwavering foundation of anti-racism and intersectional feminism. To host more inclusive and accessible events—in Nature or otherwise—we must actively choose anti-racist and feminist ways of thinking, being, and acting.

Our goal is twofold: make birding and the outdoors inclusive, affirming, and joyful to people who may not otherwise have safe access to it and support people's passion for the environment and social justice to help create lasting change.

More simply put, there is no reason why we can't celebrate birdlife and support our most cherished beliefs in equity and justice at the same time. For us, it's not either/or.

THE COLLECTIVE POWER OF "WE"

Although the two of us—Molly Adams and Sydney Golden Anderson—coauthored and curated the collection of artworks, quotes, and essays found throughout the following pages, we could not have done so without the support and shared knowledge of the extraordinary change-makers, our elders and teachers, who have been doing this work long before we began. This is the collective power of *We*. *We* stand together with those who precede us to tell this story; *We* walk this road today with so many others; and *We*—including you, dear reader—are in this together, no matter what.

SO, WHO ARE YOUR AUTHORS?

Sydney (she/her) is a grower and maker living in the Colorado Foothills on the ancestral homelands of the Ute, Arapaho, and Cheyenne. Sydney works to support communities nationally as they implement equitable conservation programs and cultivate biodiverse habitat for wildlife in their cities and neighborhoods. She loves bufflehead ducks.

Molly (she/they) is a naturalist, advocate, and conservationist from New York. After becoming disabled by COVID-19, they are learning to live, find balance, and bird in new ways, primarily in the Catskill Mountains, on stolen lands used by the Mohican, Schaghticoke, and Haudenosaunee people.

As the Feminist Bird Club founder, board member, and New York City chapter leader (Molly), and former chapter leader for FBC Chicago and FBC New York City (Sydney), we have personally witnessed the incredible benefits of creating community in Nature and advocating for all living creatures.

In tandem with our writing, you'll encounter the wisdom of numerous other birders working toward better worlds. To say we're merely grateful to offer our collectively gathered experiences as birders and organizers would be the understatement of a lifetime. It's an honor to author this book.

WHY THIS BOOK? WHY NOW?

This book was written and its information gathered as a soothing balm for the troubling times we live in.

Global struggles often feel overwhelming and sometimes completely outside our control. From the ever-evolving risk of long-term health effects from the COVID-19 pandemic; to increased physical and political violence against people of color, women, and trans, nonbinary, and disabled folks; to the escalating reality of climate crisis (another kind of violence), especially for women, children, Black, Brown, disabled and/or low-income peoples globally—these issues are massive.

One thing we understand is that every prevailing injustice upon the Earth and its inhabitants is interconnected, each reliant upon the existence of the other. There is hope in knowing that as many of us tug upon our work in the world, it inevitably helps unravel the systems that keep all beings from thriving.

This book aims to unravel the threads at the intersection of birding and community. We desire to hold space for global sufferings and provide pathways for connections and small-scale solutions. Within the following pages, you will learn more about FBC's methods for doing just that. You will find a list of Feminist Bird Club principles; next, a glossary, intentionally located at the book's beginning so that we arrive together with equal understanding. Throughout the book, you'll encounter artworks by diverse makers that communicate the vital role of emotional response and culture in igniting change. And finally, you'll read four essays meant to guide you through the process of cultivating worlds more mindful, inclusive, reciprocal, and joyful by birding in community.

We don't pretend to be the ultimate authority on any of these subjects. There are myriad ways to pursue what this book aims to offer, and that is precisely why we need one another. The conditions we live within—whether good or bad—originate from collective imagination, fabricated and reproduced via story, policy, and action. Combining our manifold visions of futures more just and livable make us better equipped to co-create them.

With that thought in mind, intertwined with our writing, you will find journal prompts and blank pages for you to enter your wisdom right into the book—to co-create this work with us and all of the visionary folks who contributed to this volume—so that you may activate what you know to be true for you, and share it with others.

Above all else, we want this book to be a space for you to reflect on joy and connection in your own life and beyond. In the words of Dr. Ayana Elizabeth Johnson and Dr. Katharine K. Wilkinson in their anthology *All We Can Save*, "we want to tip toward community, care, repair, and renewal. We want to tip toward life."

And we want you to help lead the way forward—all the while saying: let's go birding for a better world.

FEMINIST BIRD CLUB PRINCIPLES

The following principles were written by Feminist Bird Club board members Molly Adams, Jeana Fucello, Martha Harbison, Akilah Lewis, and Karla Noboa in 2020.

→ Our feminism must focus on addressing intersectional struggles. Our work centers the experiences of, and fights for the rights of, people who identify as Indigenous, trans, nonbinary, queer, women, disabled, Black, Brown, neurodiverse, or any combination thereof, and for the equity of people from all socioeconomic backgrounds. All FBC chapters need to work against perpetuating white feminism and any extension of misogyny.

→ Our fight for conservation and environmental justice is intimately connected with the feminist and anti-racist movements. Our members must respect that these international struggles are central to our fight to address the current climate crisis.

→ At all FBC events, everyone must be respectful of one another. This includes being considerate of new birders, acknowledging an individual's pronouns, and rejecting any racist, sexist, ableist, classist, homophobic, sizeist, or xenophobic behaviors.

→ All flora, fauna, and funga encountered at events must be treated with respect, and participation in local conservation actions are always encouraged. The American Birding Association code of ethics must be followed by all members at all events.

→ We recognize that support needs to go beyond having a platform, and in order to effect change we need to provide material support, time, and labor to fight against oppression and climate catastrophe. We invite all people to join us in this work.

GLOSSARY:
ARRIVING TOGETHER

This glossary is an attempt to help everyone start from the same place. It's also important to acknowledge that the following concepts were developed by Black and Indigenous women and other people of color, queer folks, and disabled people, who have generously and boldly paved this path. Our work is not possible without theirs.

As authors, we approached this book with our unique and limited understanding, so our glossary is inevitably incomplete. In the blank pages that follow, please help us create and complete the glossary by defining any terms or concepts you think are necessary when striving for better worlds.

Accessibility: The Google dictionary definition of accessibility is "the quality of being easy to obtain or use" and/or "the quality of being easily understood

or appreciated." The ways we refer to accessibility in this book both includes and goes beyond these simple definitions. When we refer to accessibility, we also do so with the intention of incorporating frameworks of disability justice. In other words, we aim to amplify interdependence, eliminate ableism, limit barriers, and expand psychological and physical safety for all people.

Anti-racism: Anti-racism is the avid and everyday commitment to combating racism in every way possible. To be "not racist" is a passive self-appointed trait, whereas to be anti-racist implies action taken in the struggle against racism.

Birding code of ethics: We strive to always adhere to the basic principles of ethical birding developed by the American Birding Association: 1) Respect birds and their environments, 2) Respect the birding community and its individual members, and 3) Respect other humans.

Environmental justice: **Attention was first brought to issues of environmental justice by Hazel M. Johnson** of Chicago's South Side in 1977. Ms. Johnson is known as the Mother of Environmental Justice for being one of the first outspoken advocates against the unequal burden caused by environmental degradation—such as poor air quality or polluted waterways—for Black, Brown, global women, disabled folks, and low-income communities. Environmental justice applies to both the health of the Earth and human populations and seeks to establish that all people have the right to healthy ecosystems.

Intersectional feminism: **The term "intersectionality" was coined by American law professor Kimberlé Crenshaw in 1989** as "a prism for seeing the way in which various forms of inequality often operate together and exacerbate each other." Born from the lack of representation for Black, Brown, queer, and trans women in the 1840s to 1970s feminist movements, intersectional feminism acknowledges that global women are not free until all peoples of all identities are free. Intersectional feminism understands that all forms of inequality are interlocking, compounding, and happening simultaneously and works to root out the causes of all oppression.

Inclusivity: We aim to organize events in Nature with diverse populations in mind and create welcoming and affirming environments so that all participants feel safe, heard, and valued.

Joy: To feel and experience joy is different for all people, but to *choose* joy—and share it with others—is one of the most important and radical forms of resistance we can utilize in the face of compounding injustice and global crises.

Leisure privilege: Access to resources like money, time, and physical and emotional ability allows one to enjoy free—not working—time. Many disabled and working people around the globe are not afforded the same luxury because of an inequitable lack of access and preventative barriers.

Nature: We aim to honor myriad Indigenous ways of being that celebrate humans' coevolution with all living organisms. Our use of the word Nature as a proper noun, capitalized throughout the book, is meant to evoke and honor knowledge-ways that have been too often invalidated and, in many cases, eradicated, by colonial violence.

So-called United States: The United States was founded on the enslavement of African peoples, the historic and present exploitation of the working class, and the continual attempted genocide of Indigenous societies in order to steal and decimate their lands. The phrase "so-called" acknowledges that this land was (and still is) many things before it became the United States. We use "so-called" as a way of reckoning with our collective pasts to inform our futures and ask tough questions like *How can we hold harmful systems accountable? How can we do differently by each other and the Earth?*

JOURNAL PROMPT

What terms or concepts are important
to you when you envision worlds
more just, livable, connected,
and joyful? Define them here. We'd
love to learn how you define better
futures for everyone. If you'd like
to share your responses with FBC,
please go to feministbirdclub.org/
birdingforabetterworld, or post your
response on social media using the
hashtag #BirdingForABetterWorld and
tagging @feministbirdclub.

CHAPTER ONE

THE BASICS OF BIRDING

FINDING STILLNESS AND LOOKING CLOSELY

B IRDING IS DEFINED as the simple act of enjoying wild birds. This inclusive definition originates from Freya McGregor, cofounder of Birdability (@BIRDABILITY), a disability justice birding organization. Following their lead, Feminist Bird Club has moved away from using the term "bird watching" because you do not need to physically see birds to enjoy them.

Birding may not be everyone's passion, but we believe it has the capacity to enhance your experience of the world by encouraging you to mindfully experience the everyday places you inhabit.

If you're new to birding, this chapter is for you.

WHAT BROUGHT MOLLY TO BIRDING?

I began birding around 2012 after being diagnosed with a health condition that required me to minimize stress in my life. I had just spent four years studying art, ecology, and museums in busy New York City when I took a life-changing trip (where I saw waved albatrosses!) that made me want to capture the excitement and wonder of being in a new place and infuse it into my everyday life.

Soon after, I moved back to the calm, coastal shores of Long Island, New York, where I had the privilege of growing up. During summers, my family and I spent most of our time together around the ocean with lots of beach-nesting birds. One of my first bird-related memories is of helping a tern chick that was stuck in a tire track on the sand.

While living on Long Island as an adult, I worked at a natural history museum that encouraged visitors to think like a naturalist in order to build a deeper connection to local habitats and species. My kind colleagues took me to their favorite ponds, beaches, and meadows, lent me binoculars, and taught me to identify birds based on their behaviors, the seasons, and where they were seen. I became instantly absorbed in this new hobby, which required me to find stillness and be present while gently pushing me to unravel and appreciate the levels of interconnectedness of birds, places, climate, and time.

This experience drove me to pursue a master's degree in conservation and begin assisting research on and advocacy for the same beach-nesting bird species I scooped out of the sand twenty years prior.

Birding allowed me to reconnect to seemingly familiar landscapes, infusing them with more meaning and inspiration for action. Best of all, I could bring this tool with me wherever I went. Birds are everywhere!

I moved back to New York City a few years later, and birding completely transformed my relationship to the city. I had an unwelcoming experience in Central Park with a birding guide that made me hesitant to join existing groups, but I wanted nothing more than to share my feelings and motivation to be involved in conservation and my community. So, the Feminist Bird Club was formed!

HOW DID SYDNEY FIND BIRDS?

At the age of fourteen, I was taken in by my paternal grandmother and moved from Dallas, Texas, where I was born, into my Grammy's home in the Piedmont region of North Carolina. I found much needed respite in the tall, tall pines and many hummingbird feeders, bluebird boxes, and birdbaths tucked into the contours of Grammy's small backyard. She could often be found shouting from the kitchen with glee, pointing toward the window with the blinds drawn high: "Look! An American goldfinch! And there— a Carolina wren!"

I'll never forget the day she told me that in another life, one where she wasn't pressured into domesticity at nineteen, she would have pursued a career as an ornithologist.

I began looking closely at birds because of my Grammy, and my appreciation for feathered friends only increased as I moved to the verdant Blue Ridge Mountains of

western North Carolina to pursue an under-graduate degree in ecology. While there, I learned what it meant to fiercely love the Earth with the entirety of my identity.

After a couple of years in wildlife conservation and nonprofit work, I moved to Chicago for graduate school and became involved with Feminist Bird Club, first as a participant and later as a chapter coordinator. FBC allowed me to practice birding and being with Nature in a renewed way. For the first time, I felt like it was more than okay to not be an expert at the thing I loved to do. There were other women and queer people from this joyful and affirming bird community to show and explain birds to me, to open my eyes to the marvel of *just looking*. It was only then that I was able to relax into the process of simply enjoying wild birds.

In the absence of self-inflicted anxiety around mis-identifying the flying creatures soaring high, wading through the river, or foraging for seeds from the tall prairie grass, I began to genuinely appreciate birds. And I became better able to identify them, too.

JOURNAL PROMPT

What inspired you to begin birding?
And/or, what is it about birding
or spending more time in Nature
that appeals to you?

USEFUL BIRDING TOOLS

There are many pieces of equipment that you can use while birding to enhance your experience. Binoculars are the most recommended item; they can quite literally open your eyes to new birds and details about them that you couldn't have observed otherwise. Monoculars are also especially useful for birding on the go, as they come in sizes small enough to store in your everyday bag or backpack.

Although heavy and usually quite expensive, spotting scopes are wonderful for looking at birds from a distance. They can be useful for birders with limited mobility and for observing owls, seabirds, shorebirds, and waterfowl—some of these species tend to remain still for longer periods of time.

Don't be afraid to bring things with you that might make birding easier. For birders with difficulty walking or standing, consider bringing a camping stool or lightweight chair if you're unsure if a site will have ample benches. Additional gear is necessary for some birders, but a nice place to rest can be appreciated by anyone.

Early morning birding during peak migration or a trip to a crane congregation site can be an exciting and powerful experience to take in through multiple senses. If you're prone to auditory overstimulation, consider packing earplugs or noise-canceling headphones.

While birding on your own, or with other beginners, a guidebook or bird app can help you understand more about what you're experiencing. David Sibley and Roger Tory Peterson both wrote comprehensive guides with illustrations and field notes for all the species one might find in so-called North America. You can also find regional guides to make it easier to narrow down your identifications. *North American Birdwatching for Beginners*, by Sharon Stiteler, is another option that covers the basics of identifying 150 common bird species. (To put this number into perspective, there are over 11,000 known bird species found across the globe!)

You can also choose from numerous other birding guides that are more localized and broken down by state or groups of birds, often packaged as lightweight folding pocket guides that are easily transportable in the field.

One of our go-to apps for identifying birds is Merlin Bird ID, from the Cornell Ornithology Lab, and downloadable for free wherever apps are found. Merlin Bird ID has multiple helpful features that make identifying birds in your ecoregion by sight, habitat, season, calls, and songs almost completely effortless.

Another digital resource and community-science database is eBird, which is updated in real time and available around the globe for birds seen within a particular area. For example, let's say you live in Albuquerque, New Mexico, and plan to go birding at El Oso Grande Park later in the afternoon. You can check eBird for recent sightings and use the app to keep track of the different species you see while in the field.

Sometimes guidebooks can be cumbersome and apps a bit overwhelming. If you'd like to leave these tools at home, we recommend bringing a notebook and writing implement to jot down any impressions that birds make on you. You can always revisit your notes and consult the guides at a later time.

BINOCULAR TIPS AND TRICKS

Locating a bird in binoculars can be a bit tricky at first. The best method we've found is to begin by scanning the trees for birdy movements, as well as looking on the ground or in the sky or water. Then, lock your eyes on the bird and bring the binoculars directly to your eyes without taking your sight off the bird. Another fun technique for spotting birds is to slowly scan the environment using your binoculars. Doing so can lead to some unexpected sightings for birds camouflaged in the landscape.

WHERE CAN YOU BIRD?

Birding can be done practically anywhere! Backyard birding can be easily accessed, and installing a feeder in the yard, on your porch, or outside your window is a wonderful way to become familiar with the birds inhabiting or passing through your local environment. In some cases, depending on time of year and where you're located, you might have a few dozen or more species visit the feeder. Otherwise, you can bird while in your neighborhood or community park, or from your apartment balcony. Birding is possible while riding in the passenger seat of a car, biking in the countryside, or through the bus window on your daily commute. And with access to a vehicle and leisure privilege, you can bird in more remote places like designated conservation areas, backcountry settings, wildlife preserves, state parks, national parks, or national forests.

BIRD HABITATS

When and where you find a bird, and its behavior, can tell you a lot about what species it might be. Many birds migrate from one region or habitat to another according to the seasons. Range maps that show you where a species would typically be at certain times of the year are usually included in most guides and apps.

Because our readers live across many different ecoregions, we thought it would be most useful to cover types of birds often found within generalized habitats or locations. We also included some of what these birds eat, because if you know what an animal enjoys, you'll know where to look for them.

For example, if you're inland and see a large shadow and look up to see a bird soaring above, it is likely a bird of prey such as a red-tailed hawk, golden eagle, or turkey vulture. Raptors benefit from high vantage points while soaring and spotting small mammals for their next meal—alive for the hawk and eagle, and freshly dead carrion for the vulture. Or perhaps what you see flying high is a corvid such as the common raven or American crow, who are opportunistic feeders, meaning they'll eat almost anything. If you're on or near the ocean, however, it's likely a large seabird: a brown pelican, a northern gannet, or maybe even a magnificent frigate bird, searching for fish over the sea. It could also be a bird of prey that eats fish, like an osprey or bald eagle.

Let's say you're sitting on a park bench and there are birds on the grass or fluttering in the trees; you are most likely observing songbirds that may be looking to snack on insects, seeds, or fruit. Songbirds seen on the ground might be American robins, a couple of dark-eyed juncos, or a small group of indigo buntings. If it's springtime and the songbirds are tiny, quick-moving, and often brightly colored, they likely belong to a wood-warbler species—like a northern parula or Nashville warbler flitting after flying insects. If you're in a botanical garden and see a small bird hovering in an unusual manner or zipping between flowers, that's a hummingbird drinking nectar—there are over 330 species of hummingbirds globally!

Near a body of water? If the bird is swimming, it's likely a waterfowl, like a ruddy duck, bufflehead, mallard, cinnamon teal, Canada goose, or maybe a trumpeter swan, who either dive under or dabble on top of the water for their meals.

If the bird is standing still on the banks or walking on long, thin legs through the reeds, stalking their aquatic prey, it

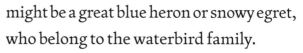 might be a great blue heron or snowy egret, who belong to the waterbird family.

Along the coast, birds dashing between and around waves or nesting in the dunes are likely shorebirds, perhaps an American oyster-catcher or black-bellied plover foraging for small bivalves and invertebrates buried in the sand.

Species you might find on the ground in more arid regions could include the notorious greater road-runner chasing after a lizard, or the unreasonably cute California quail munching on leaves. And finally, some backyard birds on or around feeders—in the Western US, specifically—could include the spotted towhee, lesser goldfinch, Anna's hummingbird, black phoebe, acorn woodpecker, Bewick's wren, yellow-rumped war-bler, and so much more.

PLUMAGE AND SONG

One thing that makes birds difficult to identify is that most of them fly, and many of them fly quickly. As a result, although birds' general habitat requirements are true much of the time, they can some-times be found doing unexpected things in unexpected places, and they might not remain still long enough for you to get a good look at them.

Birds' plumage—the colors and patterns of their feathers—can also change, depending on the season and the age of the bird. Male and female birds, especially songbirds, are often sexually dimorphic; in other words, they look quite different from one another. Some male birds will display showy, bright colors and sing their loudest during their breeding season while trying to find a mate. When migratory birds return south for the winter, the same male birds will typically molt their showy plumage and can more closely resemble their female counterparts.

Birds' flighty personalities and variation in plum-age is why learning birdsong can be useful. The best advice we have for learning bird vocalizations is to sit still on a spring day, listen closely, and try to connect the sounds you hear to the birds you see. Many bird guides include charming mnemonics such as "Who cooks for you? Who cooks for you all?" for the barred owl, and "teacher, teacher, teacher, teacher" for the ovenbird as it rises to a crescendo. There are lots of variations of these fun tools. For example, some people hear the ovenbird screaming "pizza, pizza, pizza, pizza," so feel free to make up your own.

Over time, you'll remember that the buzzy set of trills belongs to a blue-winged warbler and that northern cardinals really do sound like they're shooting laser beams. Listening to recordings of songs and calls when you're back from birding may also be useful for learning sounds for identification purposes. The various apps (Merlin Bird ID, for example) that include features that pick up on sounds can also help you put songs to species. Remember that just like humans, sometimes this new technology can make mistakes.

Determining specific bird species can be dependent on quite a few things; but we hope this overview gives you a point of reference to begin from. Your bird-identification journey may seem overwhelming at first; however, the closer you look, the easier this exciting endeavor becomes. Try starting with what's present in your local environment and move outward from there. At any point, if you get frustrated with figuring out which species you saw or heard, gently remind yourself that you don't need to be able to identify a bird to enjoy being in their presence. And remember, there are over eleven thousand species of birds around the world—there's always something new to learn.

DEBUNKING BIRDING MYTHS

→ Birding does not mean "bird walk." **In fact, you don't have to walk at all while birding. This kind of birding is often called a "sit." Staying rooted in one place and waiting for birds to make their appearance can be a meditative and deeply enjoyable experience.**

→ Birding isn't inherently competitive.

→ Birding doesn't have to be a solo experience; **you can share it with friends, family, and community.**

→ Birding is for people of all ages. **Even babies will marvel at the sight of birds.**

→ Common birds—like house sparrows and rock pigeons—are cool too! **Common species are particularly well-adapted, often called generalists, for their ability to survive and thrive in all kinds of circumstances.**

→ You can bird at any time of day—**not just at dawn, dusk, and late at night, when some birds are most active. Although birdy activity might slow down during the hottest parts of the day, birds are always around.**

→ You don't have to have fancy or expensive equipment to begin birding. **It's about being outside and using your senses to enjoy birds.**

→ Birders often love sharing the wonders of birds with others. **If you see someone looking through binoculars or a spotting scope and are curious about what they see, it's definitely okay to thoughtfully ask them.**

→ Yes, you're a birder, even if you're not an expert. **You don't even need to correctly identify birds to call yourself a birder. There's no singular way to enjoy wild birds.**

JOURNAL PROMPT

Can you remember the first bird
you were able to identify? What was
it called? Can you remember where
you were, what you were doing, what
it felt like to identify a bird for
the first time?

BIRDING AS MEDITATION

Meditation is an ancient practice that exists across numerous cultures and means many different things to different people. It is often considered a way of connecting with yourself in the present moment through reflection and stillness. People meditate to find a moment of calm in their busy lives or to cultivate an overall sense of peace over time. This quiet period of reflection can gently lead to new levels of understanding of yourself and the world.

Traditionally, meditation is practiced while sitting, lying down, or slowly moving while focusing on your breath or guided contemplation points. When you meditate outside or by a window, you can create space to connect more deeply with yourself and the miraculous dance of Nature unfolding all around you. Birding itself requires patience and stillness, but it also requires our attention. As you spend more time practicing mindfulness in any outdoor environment, you come to know different species, what habitats they prefer, and what times of the year you can and can't observe them. This encourages a deeper knowledge of the seasons and your local habitats.

Bridget Butler, a birder and naturalist who coordinates with the FBC Northern Vermont chapter, teaches a method of mindfulness-focused birding that she calls "slow birding." This practice explores an approach to observing birdlife focused on reawakening and fine-tuning your innate senses, while at the same time creating a deeper connection to yourself and the place you live.

Mindful birding can also have a profound impact on the quality of our lives and mental well-being. In the moving words of Tammah Watts from her stunning book *Keep Looking Up: Your Guide to the Powerful Healing of Birdwatching*:

With practice, my ability to mindfully be with birds increased. During extremely difficult times when I was consumed by depressing thoughts, physical pain, and stress, I would step outside and search the sky. At times I would follow a hawk as it soared high overhead, next to a vast canyon. As the bird rose on the air's currents, I would slowly breathe in and out in united reverence. The higher it ascended, the deeper my breathing became, allowing my body much-needed relaxation and alleviation of anxiety.

Spending time in awe of Nature can be a powerful antidote to hopelessness and despair. There's something restorative about remembering how we simultaneously evolved for a hundred and fifty thousand years alongside all life-forms right outside our doorsteps. When we feel connected—to the birds, to the land, to each other—it helps us remember who and what we are: sentient animals that require unbridled sunlight and fresh air, clean water, and nutritious foods.

As we collectively awaken to centuries of colonial and capitalist abuse of the land, animals, and global peoples, mindful birding can be a tool within our toolbox for building something better. Perhaps when we bird with intention and stillness, we can remember how much we stand to lose.

PNATMUIKU'S WULO'NUK - 07/04/2020
WISAWOQSIT?

JOURNAL PROMPT

The next time you go birding,
if it feels right, set your
phone to silent. Try to minimize
distractions. Find a comfortable
seat and begin to place an emphasis
on your breath. Breathe in through
your nose for a count of four, hold
for two, then breathe out through
your mouth for a count of eight.
Feel free to modify this breathing
technique to your needs.

———

As long as you feel comfortable
connecting with your body in this
way, make an effort to breathe
mindfully throughout the entire

birding meditation. Try not
to judge yourself if you lose
count of the breath.

———

If focusing on your breath in this
way does not feel right for you,
attempt to solely focus on the
second part of the meditation:
gently make note of the different
sounds or signs of movement in
your environment. Then, let the
happenings in your environment—
the birds flying overhead, small
mammals scuttling up a tree,
insects buzzing by, ants on the
cuff of your sleeve, all the
miniscule and marvelous parts of
Nature—come to you. Take note
of what's there.

CHAPTER TWO

BETTER BIRDING

INCLUSIVITY AND
ACCESSIBILITY
IN THE OUTDOORS

Before we encourage folks from historically excluded communities to rush unhesitatingly into the outdoors, I want us to remember that safety, access, and inclusivity don't just enhance our joy in Nature; I strongly believe that they are the prerequisites to experiencing joy.

—**Meghadeepa Maity**, FBC Director of Accessibility and Intersectional Community Engagement

BIRDING CULTURE cannot be excluded from critiques and conversations on race, class, ableism, and heteropatriarchy. Birding is for everyone, but the history of birding in colonized North America has not always reflected that truth. Until recently, those with authority in birding have almost always been able-bodied white men, while nearly all others were excluded from birding or positions of leadership within ornithology. Some birds are even named after European and North American naturalists of the mid-to-late 1800s with problematic pasts as agents of colonialism, eugenics, slavery, and white/male supremacy. Just as Confederate monuments topple across the United States, efforts to rename birds and make experiences in Nature more inclusive and accessible are well underway.

It's relevant to ask: How do we, in the collective sense, do more than just claim to be inclusive for people of intersecting identities? We're discovering that the answer does not come easily if given authentically. It is ever-evolving as we grow and learn as individuals, as a collective cultural body, as a nonprofit. In essence, we can't provide a formula for making events in Nature more inclusive and accessible.

At best, we can learn from our mistakes, and we can uplift what we've learned from our community of intersectional birders. As FBC endeavors toward a more equitable world, we are constantly reminded that there are countless other individuals, clubs, and organizations also doing this work in many ways. On page 143 you'll find a list of other radical Nature-based organizations we're proud to know. Give them a follow and join the work that feels right for you.

STRIVING TOWARD MAKING BIRD EVENTS MORE ACCESSIBLE

If you're the organizer of an event, keep in mind that language can be important when you're designing accessible birding experiences or other outdoor programs. Advertising experiences in the field as a "bird trip" or "outing" rather than "bird walk" or "bird watch" sets a tone of inclusivity for physically disabled folks or people with vision impairments.

Detailing each event's logistics is equally imperative when designing accessible bird outings. It's important to specify types of trail surfaces (gravel, sand, paved, wheelchair accessible); trail length, type, gradient (for example, 0.75 miles, out-and-back, flat); places to rest; whether binoculars are provided; whether bathrooms are available and if accessible stalls are present; and whether face masks are required when social distancing isn't possible during the ongoing pandemic.

Details regarding transportation to and from the site are also highly useful; for example, whether public transit is an option. And lastly, specifying the maximum number of participants allotted for the event can be significant for folks with post-traumatic stress disorder (PTSD), sensory sensitivity, and/or social anxiety. As you continue to learn about your participants' needs, this list will likely grow.

In addition to designing bird outings with disabled folks in mind, you could offer virtual events for those with limited access to in-person experiences. The COVID-19 pandemic has made the availability of these kinds of programs even more necessary, especially for people who need or desire to stay home while the pandemic affects the most vulnerable in our communities.

To make online events as accessible as possible, record your events, include closed captions, and provide visual descriptions when closed captions may not be enough. If you're able to, include American sign language and other language translation options. Invite attendees to let you know if there are any access needs they would like to share with you so that you can try your best to accommodate them.

While no event will ever be inclusive of everyone all of the time, working toward the most accessible programming possible helps us to learn about each other and grow together.

JOURNAL PROMPT

Describe an event you've attended or an activity that you've participated in that did or did not meet your personal-access needs. What aspects of the event made you feel at home? What could have made you feel more supported and included?

"Birders are as infinitely diverse as Nature. An inclusive birding community should reflect that diversity. My ideal birding community intentionally addresses and removes the barriers that restrict access to the hobby and remains accountable for future transgressions."

—**Danielle Belleny**, author of *This Is a Book for People Who Love Birds*

INCLUSIVITY IN THE OUTDOORS

Our goal as an organization and as individuals has always been to make everyone feel welcome and a part of the outdoors while prioritizing the safety and inclusion of birders from historically marginalized or excluded groups. We do this, and so can you, through intentional language choices, outreach, and a conscious attitude during programming. Our event leaders strive to be kind and approachable, and they emphasize that we are all collectively learning about and enjoying wild birds rather than follow a more traditional "expert" model that dictates information to a silent group of followers.

If you're organizing any kind of programming around birding, whether in-person or virtual, consider making it free and/or donation-based if possible. At FBC events, binoculars are also typically available to borrow, along with a lesson on how to use them. Ideally, it's important to never turn someone away from an event for financial reasons.

Paying leaders rather than asking folks to donate their time is also a significant contribution to generating more inclusive events. Since Feminist Bird Club first received funding for the New York City chapter in 2019, paying event leaders became a priority. This has allowed us to hire BIPOC, chronically ill, and/or queer birders to host our events and model for new birders with similar intersectional identities that the experiences are for them.

We also recommend starting your birding trips with a land acknowledgment. This can consist of mentioning that you're honored to bird on the homelands of the Munsee Lenape people (in Manhattan specifically) and expressing gratitude for the past and present Indigenous people who have stewarded the land.

Consider also encouraging a deeper conversation about the Indigenous history of every local environment you visit. This may mean researching and discussing the history of the land, and connecting with the Indigenous nations nearby and supporting their contemporary work.

In New York City, we are honored to learn from Haley Scott, an Afro-Caribbean, Afro-Latina, and Indigenous (Unkechaug Indian Nation) bird guide and chapter leader who begins her land acknowledgments in Algonquian as a way to combat Indigenous erasure. Haley also includes Indigenous place names and local knowledge that Munsee and Lenape relatives have shared with her in order to provide important precolonial histories that are largely ignored.

You can visit www.native-land.ca as a jumping off point to learn about the Indigenous people of your region.

You might also find it useful to ask participants to share, if they feel comfortable, their names, pronouns,

and any access requirements that they'd like the group to know about before beginning to bird.

FBC trip leaders regularly share things they might need assistance with during the event—like birdsong or visual identifications for species they're unfamiliar with—to really emphasize that everyone learns from one another when birding in community, and that birding expertise isn't accumulated linearly. There is so much to learn about ecosystems and bird behavior without ever knowing the Western prescribed names for any species.

WE TAKE CARE OF EACH OTHER

In the springtime of 2020, there quickly arose unprecedented numbers of people seeking experiences in Nature and connecting outside as a way to cope with everyday stresses and pandemic life. Organizations like Flock Together (@FLOCKTOGETHER.WORLD) and BlackAFInStem (@BLACKAFINSTEM) were also emerging around the same time. Flock

Together is a United Kingdom–based birding collective for people of color. Their impact—along with other BIPOC-focused birding groups—has rippled across the globe. BlackAFInSTEM's work centers Black excellence, experience, and joy in the sciences, culminating in a weeklong birding celebration known as Black Birders Week. But even while incredible organizations like Flock Together and BlackAFInStem form and thrive, in comparison to white counterparts, Black Americans are nearly 3.3 times more likely to be harassed, harmed, or even killed by police while walking, sleeping, spending time with family, living, breathing, birding.

White people: we cannot look away from the harmful conditions white-supremacist violence has created.

A poignant example of a related incident within the birding community, which inspired Black Birders Week, was the experience of Chris Cooper, who was accosted by a white woman while birding on a spring day in 2020. (The same horrible day, May 25th, that George Floyd was murdered by police in Minneapolis.)

Chris was birding in an area of New York's Central Park called the Ramble when he asked a woman to leash her dog.  Although dogs are allowed off-leash in parts of Central Park, the Ramble isn't one of those places because it is managed for conservation purposes. Within conservation areas, dogs must be on-leash as they can harm wildlife by causing undue stress and disturbing nests.

The woman denied his request, called the police, and accused Chris of threatening harm to her and her dog. The history of white women making false claims against Black men in the United States percolates throughout time; the pattern of aggression hasn't ended.

And although Chris recorded the entire incident and thankfully left the scene physically unhurt, we'd be remiss if we didn't consider how the incident would have differed if a bystander had stepped in. When bystanders recognize and intervene in harassment situations and center the need of the person experiencing harm, we are significantly more likely to stop trauma from happening, keeping our friends and neighbors safe. Here's what you can do if you see someone experiencing harassment anywhere:

Document: **Record or take detailed notes while the incident is taking place. Thorough notes can be helpful in the event the person being harassed wants documentation for any reason. Before utilizing this tactic, note if the person being harassed is already being helped. If not, utilize one of the other options listed here. Remember to always ask for consent before sharing the content of your documentation with anyone. In some places, it is illegal to record an incident without the consent of all parties; look into the regulations of your specific area to be best prepared.**

Distract: **Distract the person perpetrating the harassment by any means necessary. You can spill your coffee or make a loud sound. Any distracting scene could redirect the harasser's attention away from the victim.**

Delegate: Delegation means asking for assistance while intervening in harassment. Assess who might be able to help—often a great choice is a person right next to you. This can mean asking an authority figure (such as an event leader or public-transit personnel) to step in, but contacting law enforcement should be a last resort.

Direct: Directly confront the person conducting the harassment by calling out their behavior. This method is to be used with extreme caution. Importantly, ask yourself first: Am I physically safe? Is the person being harassed physically safe? Is the situation likely to escalate?

Delay: Sometimes an incident happens too quickly to intervene in real time. If that's the case, you can still make a difference by checking in on the person in need of support. Even simply acknowledging their experience by saying something like "I saw that—are you okay? Can I do anything for you?" can have a positive impact.

LEARNING, UNLEARNING, LEANING ON EACH OTHER

———

Each of us begins right where we are and nowhere else. Community work will likely never be perfect—we're fallible and flawed, every one of us. The best we can hope for is to minimize any harm done while putting as much goodness and grace into our enormous yet surprisingly small, interconnected ecosystems. But the permission to try and fail and do better next time does not negate the very real and serious work ahead. It's important to remember to scrutinize our privileges and work intersectionally to dismantle all notions of supremacy and other forms of violence. We must ask for help when we need it and accept feedback for the generous gift that it is.

We must also remember there are small-scale solutions to the most pressing challenges of our time already present across all spaces and communities. We already have all the answers and technologies needed to

generate just and livable futures—
and we're not at it alone.

And while each of us is accountable for creating the world we wish to be
part of, our bodies and nervous systems are not made to
withstand the relentless waves of devastation regularly
appearing in our news cycles and social media pages.
As we feel the ache of the world and breathe life into
renewed possibility for better futures, we are *also* to be
idle, to do nothing, to look at the birds, and to love the
Earth. Don't you, too, feel a bit more hopeful after a long
nap in the sun, birds singing overhead?

JOURNAL PROMPT

What will you do to make your community-oriented experiences more inclusive, affirming, and accessible to people of diverse identities and lived experiences? And/or: If you don't currently organize community events, consider how you would respond if you saw a person being verbally or physically harassed while spending time in Nature. How would you intervene?

CHAPTER THREE

BIRDING WITH CARE

ISSUES, ETHICS, AND RESPONSIBILITIES

THE HEALTH OF THE LAND, FLORA, FAUNA, and funga is at the very core of birding. It's easy to fall in love with birds, but we can cherish them and still overlook the issues that leave them in peril. Multiple factors are working against bird populations globally, such as habitat loss, climate change, collisions with buildings, and much more. Bird diversity and populations across all ecosystems are declining at a staggering rate, a heartbreaking situation for those of us who love avian critters but also ecologically calamitous. Birds are known as indicator species, much like amphibians and insects; when their populations are steady or thriving, it indicates the ecosystem is in balance. The opposite is also true.

My first experience (Sydney here) birding with FBC was in the early fall of 2019. One of my professors in graduate school told me about Feminist Bird Club. Knowing of my interest in conservation and community care, she encouraged me to attend an FBC event. I took her advice and arrived in the early morning at LaBagh Woods on the outskirts of Chicago with my nerves in a bundle, feeling both excited and anxious about birding with other people as a novice. After walking around the forest, looking and listening for birds, we spent a few hours revegetating LaBagh with native shrubs that would support bird habitat and long-term ecosystem health. The work was hard, but it felt necessary, as if it were the most reciprocal way to enjoy wild birds.

FBC Chicago is one of the many chapters that regularly partners with other organizations to promote conservation and bioregional interdependence. Habitat loss, resulting from deforestation, industrialized agriculture, over-extraction, and polluted waterways, is among one of the top challenges facing bird populations in Chicago and across the globe. On the surface it may seem obvious: the loss of land and food sources equals less space for birds to fulfill their biological needs. The more complicated story is one of entangled relationships—everything in an ecosystem evolves simultaneously. The demise of a single species can have a devastating domino effect. As we decimate biodiverse landscapes, we disrupt systems of interdependence and exacerbate extinction rates.

In fact, conservationists predict that we will lose 14 percent of global bird species by 2050. Recent reports show that one million plant and animal species are at critical risk of extinction over the coming decades due to carbon emissions and loss of healthy ecosystems, and some estimates for species' decline are equal to that of the Permian extinction, some 250 million years ago, in which 90 percent of life on Earth was lost. We are in the midst of the sixth mass extinction event in our planet's history, but this time, the patient hands of tectonic plates and geologic time are not the ones responsible.

From tropical forests to productive grasslands, coral reefs to mountain bogs, we need diverse ecosystems to prevent and mitigate anthropogenic climate change. Forested ecosystems in the United States are single-handedly responsible for 16 percent of global carbon sequestration by absorbing carbon dioxide—a leading greenhouse gas responsible for global warming—through their leaves and storing it in the soil. Meanwhile, BIPOC and low-income urban communities have disproportionately less access to Nature and tree coverage compared to white and/or affluent communities and are significantly more likely to suffer from pollution-related illnesses such as childhood asthma, certain types of cancers, and mood-disorders like depression and anxiety, further emphasizing the inequitable burden of environmental-related issues on already marginalized communities.

In the absence of robust, diverse ecosystems capable of

absorbing excess carbon released from burning fossil-fuels, the planet will continue warming at rates never seen before.

This isn't a future problem; climate change is happening now. Polar ice caps are melting, causing sea levels to rise and raising ocean temperatures. Deep oceanic currents that drive weather patterns across the land and water are being disrupted, triggering more-powerful and deadly storms. With our planet quickly warming, many birds and other species are unable to adapt swiftly enough to keep up. Climate change is the single most important issue facing life on Earth. Eliminating carbon emissions and restoring healthy ecosystems are equally imperative if we hope to save birds and humans alike.

Outdoor cats are also a huge issue for birds. Cats are responsible for the deaths of over two billion birds in the US every year. In fact, outdoor domesticated cats are the most detrimental invasive species affecting wildlife today. If you have an outdoor cat, please consider keeping your little critter indoors. Don't have a cat? Birds and frogs and other small animals still need you

XVIII. THE MOON

to advocate for them—you can do so by spreading the word and asking your friends and families to keep their cats indoors.

There are two additional major steps we can take to increase bird longevity within and around our homes and other buildings. Number one: turn off your lights at night during migration season. You can visit www.birdcast.info for migration alerts and the best times to turn off your lights. Most birds migrate at night, and the nocturnal glow of cities, large neighborhoods, and other artificially lit objects often interferes with their instinctual flight routes. Some cities are pledging to use bird migration tracking data to make their city skylines go dark in an effort often referred to as "Lights Out." Dark skies are important for the health of humans and wildlife alike, and birds especially benefit because artificial nocturnal light draws birds into urban and densely populated areas where the danger

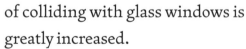

of colliding with glass windows is greatly increased.

It's difficult to describe the gut-punch feeling of finding a dead or

injured bird on the sidewalk by a city building or outside the glass window of a house or, worse, hearing or
seeing it happen. Researchers estimate that
up to one billion birds die each year
in the US from collisions with glass.
During the day, usually after a long night
of migration, birds will fly toward what looks like a safe
habitat consisting of trees and sky but is really a reflection in a window or, in the case of nonreflective glass,
the greenery or sky on the other side.

The second thing we can do to prevent collisions is
make our glass visible to birds. Thankfully, there are
several proven ways to do this. Studies have shown that
most birds will avoid flying through spaces less than two
inches high or four inches wide. To create this effect
on your windows, you can purchase ultraviolet (UV)
film and stickers and apply them to your windows.
You can also find hangable vertical cords
that break up the reflection, or get creative with a bar of soap or some paint
and draw patterns on your windows
yourself. Decals shaped like raptors,

OLIVE-SIDED FLYCATCHER

WESTERN TANAGER

ORANGE-CROWNED WARBLER

BLACK-THROATED GRAY WARBLER

EVENING GROSBEAK

PILEATED WOODPECKER

CEDAR WAXWING

unfortunately, do not work unless they are very close together, so skip buying these or other large shapes.

For apartments, offices, and community buildings, UV film can be installed. If a building is new or being renovated, contractors can use something more permanent, like glass with etched patterns, ceramic frit, or UV glaze. Glass with ceramic frit also makes heating and cooling a building more energy efficient. One might say this saves two birds with one solution.

Feminist Bird Club members in New York City and beyond have helped local Audubon chapters with advocacy and outreach to pass laws that require new buildings to use bird-safe glass and turn off their lights to reduce nocturnal lighting during migration periods. Similar efforts are igniting in other cities across North America—you or your birding group can get involved by contacting your local government, the Dark-Sky Association, or Audubon chapter.

As birders, we benefit greatly from the gifts we receive from spending time in Nature. Birds, plants, mushrooms, insects, and soil provide immeasurable offerings without asking for anything in return, but one way we can reciprocate is by treating the whole ecosystem with reverence. Sometimes birders and bird photographers neglect to consider the ways that their behavior might impact other living beings and their habitats. Being in the presence of nocturnal birds, like owls for instance, is awe-inspiring, but we must remember that these moments are a privilege and act accordingly.

Camera flashes, drones, off-leash dogs, the prolonged presence of people, and other extensions of human disturbance can cause sensitive birds to abandon entire nesting colonies and can also result in serious harm to birds or even their death. To reduce your impact, here are some suggestions to follow when around birds:

→ **Give birds space—especially if they are sensitive, endangered, or nesting species**
→ **Don't scare birds to get a better look or photo**
→ **Don't bait birds**
→ **Don't use flashes or spotlights on nocturnal species**

→ **Stay on the trail**

→ **Keep your dog on a leash or leave it at home**

→ **Avoid or minimize using recordings of bird sounds to lure them into sight**

→ **Be thoughtful when sharing exact locations on social media for rare or sensitive species**

→ **Keep a respectful volume while birding, and be mindful when "pishing"—using your voice to lure birds into view**

Potawatomi scholar and moss scientist, Dr. Robin Wall Kimmerer, writes extensively on the subject of reciprocity. In her book *Braiding Sweetgrass*, Dr. Kimmerer highlights a touching example of how pecan trees in a grove always produce pecans simultaneously. If the conditions for production are not favorable for some trees, the whole population holds off. In response to this phenomenon, she writes that "all flourishing is mutual," highlighting the idea that when we work in tandem with care and reciprocity, we can experience benefits beyond anything we can accomplish individually.

The concept of flourishing acutely relates to the practice of birding. If our primary goal as birders is to accrue extensive species lists, we lose a critical essence of birding with care. Enjoying wild birds becomes an extractive game.

Some Indigenous ways of thinking tell us that the ethics of interdependence humans embodied for thousands of years have been disrupted but not forgotten. Colonial and capitalist ideologies have taught many of us to see ourselves as separate from Nature to justify a sense of entitlement to its gifts. Capitalism encourages ceaseless and irresponsible participation in an extractive economy, and eventually endeavors us to believe the fabrication that humans are superior to all other life. As we begin to unravel and explore these muddled understandings, it is possible to remember that the opposite is true: that we are in community *with* Nature, never separate from it.

Perhaps we can also begin to recognize ourselves as gifts of the Earth, alongside the birds, trees, bugs, fruits, fungi, and all other improbable and elegant life-forms. But opening up to these notions also begs the question: What are the consequences of inaction? How can you reciprocate what the Earth has given?

Each of us holds the tremendous responsibility of borrowing the planet from future generations, of caring for the Earth and for one another. Realizing this responsibility is another gift, one that kindly grips you to say: *all flourishing is mutual.*

You belong here, and we belong to each other. Collectively, we face immense difficulty ahead, and with each interlocking crisis—from climate change to mass extinction, habitat loss to environmental injustice— it becomes increasingly clear that reciprocity is at the heart of every solution.

JOURNAL PROMPT

What initiatives to advocate for
environmental resilience are part
of your local community? How can
you get involved? Everyone has
something unique to contribute.
What skills, privileges, and gifts
do you bring to the table?

CHAPTER FOUR

BIRDING TOGETHER

FINDING JOY AND COMMUNITY IN NATURE

OBSERVATION:
From pergola to porch
post, the Northern Pygmy–
Owl flew within the field
of a dear neighbor's voice
exclaiming "look!"

OBSERVED HABITAT:
In the open dusk of
a south slanting orchard
and circumambient coastal
redwood forest.

04.24.21 ALBION, CA.

FINDING YOUR FLOCK can be a daunting task at any stage in life. As creatures of habit, we may, at times, avoid making new connections with unfamiliar people and places. Our highest hope is that this book inspires you to explore new experiences with other humans and nonhumans who make you feel seen and cared for and help you reach for futures you wish to see unfold. But we need help from our flock to earnestly advocate for birding together. Woven across the following pages are the profound words from fellow Feminist Bird Club leaders that illustrate the sense of belonging, identity, place, and joy that's made possible as you cultivate community in Nature.

My favorite part of birding with community is being able to share the feeling of joy over seemingly simple moments in Nature. If one person is excited about a bird—whether it is a bird seen in abundance or a rarely spotted species—that often rubs off onto everyone, said Frances Kane (she/her) of Chicago, IL.

Feminist Bird Club's Chapter Relations Representative, Wendy Walker (she/her) of Seattle, WA, spoke to a seemingly simple moment in Nature that expanded when experienced communally. She said, *Recently on an FBC Seattle outing, we saw two merlin fledglings ricocheting through the forest. They were chasing each other, mock-diving at a northern flicker, and (I'm guessing) feeling the pure joy of their new flight superpower. Being with a group of others whose hearts I knew also raced amplified the wonder.*

Witnessing Nature perform is a marvelous thing. How lucky we are to be alive during the most ecologically rich epoch of our planet's 4.5-billion-year lifespan. Put beautifully, Brooks Emanuel (he/they) of Durham, NC, stated that *I've always found that paying attention to the natural world has fed my empathy for everything and everyone. The more details you notice around you, the more you understand what a tiny piece of the universe you are. That, to me, is actually reassuring. It's nice to be reminded we're a part of something so much bigger.* Recognizing the miracle of being alive helps us remember what a gift it is to be here at this moment in time, co-creating the world with our human and nonhuman relatives.

When living in fast-paced, urban areas where our focus is often on individual growth and day-to-day survival, it's easy to forget the deep connections we have to one another, to Nature, and to the histories of the land a city is built upon. Haley Scott (she/her, the Bronx, NY) shared how she uses the practice of birding to deepen her relationship with all three. *As an Indigenous person, birding has allowed me to reconnect with my ancestral homelands on Sôwan Áhki (present-day Long Island) and those of my relatives in Lenapehoking (present-day New York City). Being able to share that connection with other birders who show respect and appreciation for the land has helped me to feel more confident as a woman of color and a birder.*

JOURNAL PROMPT

Locate yourself within the complex
network of life. Where are you?
Who came before you? Who are your
teachers (human and nonhuman)?

Nature gives us the space and power to locate ourselves within this complex network of life and time, to build connections with our intergenerational community, strengthen the relationship with our current selves, and shape the future.

Living through the COVID-19 pandemic while simultaneously witnessing and, in some cases, experiencing increasing political and fascist violence and the further destruction of the planet can be oppressive on the psyche. Thankfully, spending time outside helps regulate the nervous system. Nature provides an essential backdrop for dreaming up possibilities and generating restorative networks of care. Gabriela Massip Figueredo (she/her) of Jersey City, NJ, elegantly stated that, for her, *birding as part of a group gave meaning to life when the world felt so heavy...sharing Nature with others nurtures the soul and fosters a culture of care for the planet and each other.* Birding in community can recharge your batteries so that you may approach your work in the world, whatever that work may be, with a fullness of heart and a calm mind.

Alex Smolyanskaya (she/her), former San Francisco chapter lead, also emphasized the intersection of birding and change-making. She expressed that birding in community *helped me find new parts of my activist voice. It helped me find an energizing intersection between the things I loved and the positive change I wanted to make.* Alex's sentiment rings true for so many of us at FBC. And although finding joy through birding or hiking or picnicking in a meadow may not seem inherently political, no spaces or activities are neutral when our societies remain polluted by practices that preclude safety and unabashed outdoor relaxation for certain groups of people.

Try spending time in Nature with the intention of making a difference in your local ecosystem. Perhaps that intention consists of advocacy, raising funds, habitat restoration, or uplifting other organizations. For example, events planned in partnership with other local groups are some of our favorites at Feminist Bird Club, and they're a great way to build community and make meaningful change with others. Jeana Fucello (she/her), FBC treasurer based in Queens, NY, highlighted

how *wonderful it is to see different communities converging and sharing Nature together. It gives us the opportunity to hand over the reins and highlight the talents of different people.*

If you organize outdoor experiences in your community and are looking to partner with other local groups, we recommend building on the work of active organizations you admire and following their lead. If they hold meetings, consider showing up and listening to get a better sense of ways you can collaborate in earnest. Sharing resources with local libraries, LGBTQIA+ groups, refugee centers, youth organizations, and groups like Outdoor Afro (@OUTDOORAFRO) and Latino Outdoors (@LATINOOUTDOORS) can be an excellent way to expand your birding network while helping new birders feel safe and supported.

What makes you feel safe while birding in community? The answer is likely different for everyone, but FBC secretary Akilah Lewis (she/her) of Queens, NY, said that I *feel safest birding with people who allow me to be my true, authentic self.* FBC board member, Meghadeepa Maity (they/them, Western Massachusetts), responded with sincerity: *I feel safest in birding spaces that equally prioritize the well-being of birds and birders, and where I don't have to incessantly defend my values and my emotions, justify my ownership of the labels I identify with, or apologize for expressing my needs. I want all of us to be able to learn and grow together no matter where we are in our birding journeys.*

Akilah and Meghadeepa remind us of the importance of cultivating safe and brave spaces in community that expand beyond our time birding together, especially if we claim inclusivity as a core value.

Mutual aid and community care are also part of our core values, and when members of FBC have felt unstable—financially or otherwise—outside of a birding event, other birders have shown up by organizing and sharing fundraisers, deepening the roots of supportive, reciprocal relationships. How do you show up for your community?

We live in a society that doesn't make it easy to meet all of our basic needs, much less change or exist outside the boundaries and expectations imposed on us.

Deliberately forming circles that provide enough comfort and inspiration to embrace our personal and collective evolution is a momentous achievement. Being together outdoors also makes for ample opportunity to remember a fundamental principle of all things: change is constant. Compost—decay and renewal—is an ecological inevitability worth celebrating. When we walk through life with others who make us feel safe, seen, and cared for, we are given permission to compost stagnant parts of ourselves and shine bright without apology.

FBC's president Karla Noboa (they/them, Philadelphia, PA) shared their experience of birding in the warm embrace of others: *I've been able to grow confidence in who I am as an evolving person who is constantly exploring their identity. I came out as nonbinary after joining Feminist Bird Club, because I found a group of people who saw me for who I really was and supported all of me. I could finally be who I was and speak up about my beliefs and identities without judgment.*

When I'm birding with fellow gay, queer, and trans people—expressed FBC vice president Martha Harbison (they/them, Brooklyn, NY)—*I cannot help but feel safer, more open to experiencing the world around me. And every time I go out with others, I want everyone to experience that same connection, that same joy—that there's nothing more beautiful and magical in the world than to be queer, to be trans, and to live outside the boundaries of a narrow and incurious and fearful society. One memorable June day, while birding with FBC New York City and NYC Queer Birders, I looked around and saw that joy reflected on others' faces as we watched a Baltimore oriole take a bath. I wish everyone had access to that beauty and light.*

Special moments like the one that Martha described are not rarities in Nature. There is so much to be delighted by and grateful for when you lean in and look closely—especially in the company of others who allow your passions and purpose to radiate.

Small efforts like these are the first steps in generating communities, societies, and futures that work for everyone, futures where everyone is free to be exactly who they are without fear, and where each and every one of us has a stake in the health of our planet. Karla sweetly reminded us that *in spaces where you feel like you can be your whole self, you can fully give in to your inner child, you can let go, you can feel free, fully receiving the gifts that Nature gives us and the joys it brings.*

The work of loving the world is vast and full of possibility. Doing that work with others—birding and being together in Nature—is a worthwhile endeavor, one that gets us a little closer to a better world.

JOURNAL PROMPT

Find a spot where you might see a
bird taking a bath. Locate a puddle
on a hot day and watch as the
bird's feathers ruffle waywardly.
Describe your connection to the
experience. What do you notice?
How does it make you feel?

Bird Species List

RESOURCES FOR FUTURE LEARNING

Is there anything more powerful than saying I am willing to do what I can to make this world better for all living beings? Slowing down, finding joy, and connecting with others demonstrates what we may become as we reach for just and livable futures. Birding within community—with intention and care—can offer these possibilities. We thank you, from the bottom of our hearts, for being here, for loving the world, and for helping co-create this book with us through your writing and attention. Please share your contributions with us on our website at feministbirdclub.org/birdingforabetterworld, or post them on social media with the hashtag #BIRDINGFORABETTERWORLD and tag @FEMINISTBIRDCLUB. We would love to learn more about your vision for better futures.

With that, we leave you here with resources for future learning and action. If you're interested in learning more about where the ideas and motivations for this book originated, please look into the books, articles, podcasts, and websites provided below.

Birding for a Better World

BOOKS:

Belleny, Danielle. *This Is a Book for People Who Love Birds*

brown, adrienne maree. *Emergent Strategy: Shaping Change, Changing Worlds*

Johnson, Ayana Elizabeth & Wilkinson, Katharine K., editors. *All We Can Save: Truth, Courage, and Solutions for the Climate Crisis*

Kaba, Mariame. *We Do This 'Til We Free Us: Abolitionist Organizing and Transforming Justice*

Kendi, Ibram X. *How to Be an Antiracist*

Kimmerer, Robin Wall. *Braiding Sweetgrass: Indigenous Wisdom, Scientific Knowledge and the Teachings of Plants*

Lanham, J. Drew. *The Home Place: Memoirs of a Colored Man's Love Affair with Nature*

Odell, Jenny. *How to Do Nothing: Resisting the Attention Economy*

Piepzna-Samarasinha, Leah Lakshmi. *The Future Is Disabled: Prophecies, Love Notes and Mourning Songs*

Solnit, Rebecca. *Hope in the Dark: Untold Histories, Wild Possibilities*

Spade, Dean. *Mutual Aid: Building Solidarity During This Crisis (and the Next)*

Taylor, Keeanga-Yamahtta, editor. *How We Get Free: Black Feminism and the Combahee River Collective*

Watts, Tammah. *Keep Looking Up: Your Guide to the Powerful Healing of Birdwatching*

ARTICLES AND ONLINE RESOURCES:

More on Feminist Bird Club's impact: www.feministbirdclub.org/our-work

American Birding Association Code of Bird Ethics: www.aba.org/aba-code-of-birding-ethics

Bird Names for Birds: www.birdnamesforbirds.wordpress.com

Bird migration alerts: www.birdcast.info/"10 Principles of Disability Justice"

Birdability's Accessibility Map: gis.audubon.org/birdability

Indigenous lands resource: www.native-land.ca

Resources for Future Learning

J. Drew Lanham, "Nine New Revelations for the Black American Bird-Watcher," *Vanity Fair*, May 27, 2020.

10 Principles of Disability Justice: www.sinsinvalid.org/blog/10-principles-of-disability-justice

PODCASTS:

Always Be Birdin' by Samantha DeJarnett (found on all streaming platforms)

Bring Birds Back by BirdNote with Tenijah Hamilton (found on all streaming platforms)

How to Save a Planet (found only on Spotify)

On Being with Krista Tippett (found on all streaming platforms)

OTHER BIRDING AND OUTDOOR ORGANIZATIONS:

Amplify the Future, @birdersfund, www.amplifythefuture.org

BIPOC Birding Club, @bipocbirdingclubofwi, www.bipocbirdingclub.org

Birdability, @birdability, www.birdability.org

Disabled Hikers, @disabledhikers, www.disabledhikers.com

Flock Together, @flocktogether.world, www.flocktogether.world

Hike Clerb, @HikeClerb, www.hikeclerb.com

In Color Birding Club, @incolorbirdingclub, www.incolorbirding.org

Institute of Queer Ecology, @queerecology, www.queerecology.org

Latino Outdoors, @LatinoOutdoors, www.latinooutdoors.org

Mindful Birding Network, www.themindfulbirdingnetwork.com

Native Women's Wilderness, @nativewomenswilderness, www.nativewomenswilderness.org

Outdoor Afro, @OutdoorAfro, www.outdoorafro.org

Outdoor Asian, @OutdoorAsian, www.outdoorasian.com

Queer Nature, @queernature, www.queernature.org

Urban Bird Collective, www.urbanbirdcollective.org

IMAGE CREDITS

Cover illustration by Jen Lobo
Back cover art by Emily Rose Lumsdaine

SPOT ILLUSTRATIONS

Emily Rose Lumsdaine (@emily.rose. tattoos): Untitled, Digital, 2022; pp. 16, 25, 28, 30, 35, 38, 39, 40, 51, 54, 57, 62, 63, 70, 78, 85, 88, 91, 94, 105, 111, 114, 118, 122, 132, 145

Rebecca Parker: Warblers of Nova Scotia, Watercolor on paper, 2021; pp. 14, 30, 42, 45, 46, 52, 58, 67, 70, 74, 84, 89, 94, 98, 105, 109, 118, 123, 124, 131, 133, 160

Sarah Meyer (www.smeyernet.com): Untitled, Ink and watercolor on paper, 2022; pp. 15, 24, 26, 39, 45, 50, 53, 70, 75, 82, 83, 86, 90, 100, 104, 129, 130, 136, 140

p. 1: FBC logo illustrated and designed by Aidan Koch

p. 2: Companion—Platform, Fragment of *Glaucidium gnoma* (full image on p. 120)

p. 8: Krista Lee Cockrum (@lovecreatecultivate), Patchwork Birds, Acrylic on paper, 2022

p. 10: Feminist Bird Club Patches designed by Molly Adams and Corey Rubin with birds illustrated by Jennifer Kepler, Black Skimmer, 2017; Terri Nelson, Spotted Sandpiper, 2018; Annie Novak, Snowy Owl, 2019; Angie Co, Pileated Woodpecker, 2020; Liz Wahid, Yellow Warbler, 2021; Nayl Gonzalez, Belted Kingfisher, 2022; Frances Ngo, Common Nighthawk, 2023; Painted Bunting, 2016, was derived from photographs and field guide illustrations.

p. 19: Jen Lobo (@jen__lobo), Nelicourvi Weaver & Nest, Graphite and oil on paper, 2020

p. 32: Ariana Yvette Detrez (@arianadetrez), Pura Vida, Gouache on paper, 2022

GRATITUDE

We want to foremost acknowledge the hard work and dedication of each Feminist Bird Club organizer and partner there ever was, is, and will be. We are eternally grateful for the FBC community. A big, special thanks to the FBC board members and chapter leaders who graciously provided testimony behind the importance of birding in community—their thoughts are reflected throughout the final chapter.

Thank you to Martha Harbison, Karla Noboa, Danielle Belleny, Meghadeepa Maity, José Ramírez-Garofalo, and all of our critical friends who read early iterations of this work and provided essential feedback.

Thank you to Tammah Watts for being a powerful, kind, healing presence in the world.

Thank you to the nineteen artists who contributed their work to this book—Sarah Meyer, Rebecca Parker, Emily Rose Lumsdaine, Rigel Meza Richardson, Natalie Pantoja, Jen Lobo, Ariana Yvette Detrez, Companion—Platform (Lexi Visco and Calvin Rocchio), Rae Minji Lee, Kristina Wheeat, Serena Gaiela Dominguez, milo lefort, Krista Lee Cockrum, Gina Hendry, Hallye Webb, Rie Oh, Emily T. Piper, Aidan Koch, and Jen Hsu—it was an absolute pleasure working with each of you.

To Sara McKay, thank you so much for reaching out to Feminist Bird Club and initiating this book. We are forever grateful that you thought of us and facilitated the connection between FBC and Princeton Architectural Press.

A million times, thank you, to our amazing editor, Holly LaDue, for your unwavering and critical eye. And thank you, Princeton Architectural Press, for shepherding our book into the world. There's scarcely a better publishing house to call home.

I (Sydney) must thank my dear friends and fellow FBC Chicago organizers Bridget Kiernan and Frances Kane. I would not be here to write these words if it weren't for Frances and Bridget. I love you both.

Forever gratitude to my tender partner, Keven Dooley, for walking by my side through the whole of it. Thank you for encouraging my every step.

Thank you to Keven's parents, Michelle and John Dooley, for housing Keven and me in the magical Utah desert for the majority of summer 2022. There's no better backdrop for thinking and writing about birds. Thank you.

To all of the humans and nonhumans who give my life meaning—my best friends, Izzy and Laura Solomon and Elyse Fischground; my grammy and father, Marylou and Nick Anderson; my sisters and mother, Stella and Ivy White and Lucy Thornton; my river companions, Michael Perkins and TR Russ, for teaching me about freshwater fish and sleepy clams; my teachers, Drea Howenstein, adrienne maree brown, Dr. Robin Wall Kimmerer, Dr. Ayana Elizabeth Johnson, Mary Oliver, and Krista Tippett; and to my kin, the birds, bats, the black bear, the salmon, mosses, and monarchs—thank you all.

And, finally, thank you to Molly Adams for being the best collaborator in the whole wide world. Thank you for dreaming up the Feminist Bird Club and making it happen. Thank you for sharing it with us, and thank you for everything you give. You're a shining star and a gift—I'm so lucky to know you, to work with you, to call you my friend.

I (Molly) need to thank Barbara Blaisdell, Jim Ash, Frank Quevedo, Carol Crasson, and the rest of the South Fork Natural History Museum and Nature Center staff from 2012 to 2015 who so generously took me under their wings and welcomed me into the wonderful world of birding. You all changed the course of my life for the better.

To the four brave people who came birding with me on the very first Feminist Bird Club trip in October of 2016. Jen Kepler, who was my first birding friend and colleague in NYC, told me the Feminist Bird Club was a great idea and still organizes with the NYC chapter today. Nicole and Lauren, who I know are out there still enjoying birds and working to make the world a better place. And my partner in life, Corey Rubin, who has fully supported me, my love of birding, and FBC in innumerous ways from day one. Thank you especially for your creative design work on our beautiful patches and other meaningful merchandise. And for always birding with me, even when I'm too sick to stand.

Thank you to Karla Noboa, our president, chapter coordinator, and Boston chapter lead, and the first person to reach out to ask if they could start a FBC Chapter beyond NYC. It has been an honor to work alongside you, thank you for helping FBC grow and evolve to what it is today.

Thanks to Carl Safina and the Safina Center for believing in me and awarding me two years of fellowships to support the Feminist Bird Club and my other dreams.

To my parents, Sharon and Doug Adams, thank you for raising me in a place with endless marshes and beaches filled with willets, ruddy turnstones, terns, and herons. I love birding with you both. And dad, thank you for getting me my first pair of binoculars.

And of course, to Sydney, thank YOU for being the best coauthor on Earth! Without you and your phenomenal writing, this book would still just be an idea floating around. I'm so grateful to you for grounding it and bringing it life. It has been such a dream crafting this book together, and I look forward to continuing to find and share joy with you.

Notes

Notes

Notes

Notes

Notes

Notes

Notes

Notes

Notes